Inside the Storm I Want to Touch the Tremble

THE AGHA SHAHID ALI PRIZE IN POETRY

Inside the Storm I Want to Touch the Tremble

CAROLYN OLIVER

foreword by MATTHEW OLZMANN

AGHA SHAHID ALI

PRIZE IN POETRY

The Agha Shahid Ali Prize in Poetry
Published in partnership with the University of Utah
Creative Writing Program and the Guest Writers Series.

The Defiance House Man colophon is a registered trademark of
The University of Utah Press. It is based on a four-foot-tall
Ancient Puebloan pictograph (late PIII) near Glen Canyon, Utah.

LIBRARY OF CONGRESS CATALOGING-IN-PUBLICATION DATA
Names: Oliver, Carolyn, 1984– author.
Title: Inside the storm I want to touch the tremble : a poem play / Carolyn
  Oliver.
Description: Salt Lake City : University of Utah Press, [2022] | Summary:
  "Like the apiarist searching for honey in a seething hive, the poems of Inside the Storm I Want to
  Touch the Tremble, Carolyn Oliver's debut collection, are keenly aware of the world's potential for
  sweetness and sting. Girlhood's dangers echo, transmuted, in the poet's fears for her son. A body
  just discovering the vastness of "want's new acreage" is humbled by chronic illness. Epithalamion
  turns elegy. But this world that so often seems capricious in its cruelty also shelters apple orchards,
  glass museums, schoolchildren, century-old sharks; "there's no accounting for / all we want to save,
  no names." Oliver's polyphonic gathering of speakers includes lovers and saints, painters and dead
  poets, a hawk and a mother. In varied forms (ghazals and prose poems, dialogues and erasures, bref
  double and Golden Shovel, among others) these poems bear witness to and seek reprieve from
  disasters at once commonplace and terrifying. "I can't surface for every scalpel slice, / I need a
  dreamy estuary present," she writes. Stumbling toward joy across time and space, these poems hum
  with fear and desire, bewildering loss, and love's lush possibilities"-- Provided by publisher.

Identifiers: LCCN 2022005715 | ISBN 9781647690915 (paperback) |
  ISBN 9781647690908 (ebk)

Subjects: LCGFT: Poetry.
Classification: LCC PS3615.L58426 I57 2022 | DDC 811/.6--dc23/eng/20220218
LC record available at https://lccn.loc.gov/2022005715

Errata and further information on this and other titles available online at UofUpress.com

Cover: Detail of *Orpheus* by Odilon Redon, courtesy of the Cleveland Museum of Art.

Printed and bound in the United States of America.

CONTENTS

///

////

/////

\

FOREWORD

Matthew Olzmann

There's a moment near the end of the title poem in this collection where the speaker breaks the fourth wall, pivots to the reader, and says, "sometimes—it feels right to tell you this." I think the best lyric poems are interested in this type of a correspondence. They're not seeking to merely record an event. They're not intent on reporting what happened in any given situation. Instead, they're trying to forge a type of genuine, human connection with the person on the other side of this communication. They're trying to tell *you* something important or urgent. Carolyn Oliver's poems do that. They reach out to the reader and always have something to offer—some kind of yearning, ache, beauty, or dread—that's been gathered from the world around us.

And the world this poet gathers for us and draws us into can be quite profound and vast. One of the many things I admire about this excellent collection is its range. Perhaps a challenge in introducing a book like this is it can't be easily paraphrased or categorized. You can't say the book is "about this one thing." If you think it's about *X*, it's also about *Y*. It's about horses and trees and wildness and religion and patriarchy and guns and motherhood and fear and wonder. And in the same way that this collection resists categorization, the poet does as well. At various times, she is part art historian, part arborist, part witness, part cultural critic, part conduit for saints existing across time.

The expansiveness that I'm describing can also be applied to this book's emotional landscape; I love the depth and layers of feeling present here. In a time when it often seems like we're being told what to feel or how to feel, and when those prescribed modes of feeling are often simplistic or reductive, it's a privilege to encounter a poet capable of allowing many emotions and all their complications to exist next to each other in the same space. I'm reminded of Auden saying, "Poetry might be defined as the clear expression of mixed feelings." That element is immediately noticeable in this collection; it's even located in the book's title—where there's the suggestion of danger and desire, anxiety and awe—and it continually resurfaces through the poems that follow. In "Saint Ursula Advises Emily Dickinson," the speaker simultaneously feels both "unseen" and "free." The poem "Prayer" places gratitude next to terror in one line, and bliss next to rage in another. Throughout this book, the human interior is nuanced and multifaceted. Oliver writes, "Lately I've been occupied/ swallowing the world,/ every piece I can remember./ Faces, incense, music," and there's a distinct sense of an agile mind trying to do exactly that, trying to take it all in, the whole scale of being alive, *every piece*, so that she might shape those pieces into something meaningful for us.

And so, yes, it really does feel right to tell you this: *Inside the Storm I Want to Touch the Tremble* is a marvelous book and Carolyn Oliver is a poet of innumerable gifts. It's no minor achievement to illuminate the complexities of a roiling world, to reach for and hold that with grace and insight. And because she's done so, now, when you turn this page, when you enter these poems, you'll be able to hold a part of that as well.

— September 29, 2021

My Son Asks if I Would Rather Live in a House Infested by Bees or a House Infested by Koalas

Late summer: hurricane scraps batter the crabapple
that didn't bloom this year, peeling open
a paper nest high in the branches. Pitiless, I hope

it's empty, hope they're gone, the wasps.
All these hot weeks they've refused my offering
of phlox and milkweed, sunflowers and ruby

buckwheat. Instead they've stalked
the raised beds of vegetables I should tend,
patrolled the deck when I need to rest, skimmed

my neck for a flinch. Allergic too, my father
as a child had a friend whose mother died—
suffocated when a wasp, or a bee, stung her throat.

So, my son's question. Survival means
koalas on the stairs, lamps turned boughs,
menthol in the mouth. Means marked territories

and the slow click of claws in the dark, days
safe in a house full of sleep. But sometimes—
it feels right to tell you this—sometimes

inside the storm I want to touch the tremble
of a colony warming its queen. I want
walls seeping honey. I want a willing tongue.

/

Eve Grinds Pigments for Artemisia Gentileschi

The apricot lost its honeyed glow, the nettle
its hollow sting, the first time I held lapis.

    And did you ever contemplate crushing such a prize?

Only as often as I've wanted to dissolve.

    Mind you don't miss under your nails. Finer than gold
    is ultramarine—

—saved for the Virgin, I know,
though there's not so much here for a stitch in her hem.

    A stifled sigh's still
    a breath.   *Sum them,*
       make a life.

And what colors would you add for a bruise-pestled palm?

    Bloodstone. Cinnabar. Mountain ochre.
      If given a choice.
        Tell me the first color
       you remember
        as color.

Opulence, pulling in all directions.

    Tearing, I'd wager.   *I forgot,*
    no childhood.

For you: gold tested between teeth.

    Between the bed and the door, morning
    in warm winter.

Malachite next. A garden for the beheld?

A garden? No. A first
   field, for a severed head.

To the man who tried to grab my face through the car's open window

Uninvited rabbit clips clover in quick bites,
skitters under the rhododendron
when I visit the raised beds
to pluck beans, yank weeds, hum
sad Joni Mitchell songs too low
for the neighbors to hear, or the boys
bounding off the bus, loud again today,
arguing among themselves.
Under my hat I watch them head away
from the laughing girls who must live
closer to the park where I never walk alone.
Sometimes in gratitude for taking
only what it must, for giving
me wide berth, I leave yellowed basil,
lacy radish tops, or lettuce about to bolt
for the rabbit whose sex I do not know
whose eyes could be small domes of black
or the kind of brown a gardener hopes for,
that good earth color.

Waiting

1991

Maybe not only the rock

behind the man, steadying

him across from our bus stop,

this beige man safe in his

beige pants, blue cap low

over his face, haze of his

blue breath spread over

his lap, his pen and pad.

Sure of his gaze, we

three girls in red plaid.

Skin

Eighth graders on a patio, no parents home, talking together and drinking pop
(this is Ohio, the late 90s)

when one girl, the type of girl who flies under the radar, raises a languid hand
to stroke her neck

below her ear. *Isn't it weird how the skin right here feels
just like a penis?*

Not knowing if she's right, I reach for my own neck, downy, tensed,
blush-burned. Lucky girl,

I'm not afraid of our friends, the boys snorting, pretending to choke themselves.
I don't know the word *slut*,

still a few months until I begin to fathom what kind of world rewards
men intent on breaking.

Behind the girl, a dark hedge, a melon-curve of sky ripe for summer.
This is twenty years ago.

She has her own baby girl now, real sick, and the insurance company
won't approve her medicine.

The Eider Keepers

At eleven I shaved my legs for the first time,
convinced of dire necessity by sixth-grade friends
and razor ads, though in the light my shins glinted
no more than my younger brother's, and I never met
anyone who noticed the hair on a boy's legs.
Once begun the ritual demanded its own
persistence, and I came to dread the slide of soap,
the black-eyed drain gulping my hair, soft as the down
eider mothers pluck from their breasts to insulate
their seaweed nests, heavy with eggs. Come summer's end
the eiders and their chicks slip seaward, leave behind
their keepers, whose patient hands search the cobbled shacks,
barn-red huts, overturned boats—all those little havens.
In the sun they sieve the foamy down for bits of shell
and bladderwrack, harping clean the precious softness
before it's tucked away, unseen, nearly weightless,
to grace the beds of shivering smooth-skinned girls
all grown up, just waiting for someone to notice.

Saint Agnes Meets a Hawk on the River's Edge

Hawk, my lamb is lost, she says.
Her voice is a piccolo the hawk
could grip between two red talons.
Where have you lost your lamb?
The rain tastes like moss and smoke.
There is nowhere I have not lost my lamb:
in forests, in caves, in dwelling places.
The river sediment, stirred, disturbed,
remembers winter. *A bird in hand is worth*
one bird, one bird exactly. I could be
your lamb—my feathers soft as fleece.
What's the use in hunting through the storm?
The trees grow from their own martyrs.
Hawk is too familiar. The girl does not reply.
Or cannot. Her hair grows and grows,
enough to make a rope to the other shore,
or a nest.

Reading Szymborska under a Harvest Moon

Though I don't know a word of Polish,
or even how to pronounce the consonants
bunched like root vegetables, or variables,

I adore her poems offered this way:
the spine's shadowed curve a double tilde dividing
original and English versions, like scrolling

algebra equations the teacher checks, years ago,
that September I spend hoping to grow unnoticed
among the rows of desks, while behind me the window,

open against the heat, flaunts its tantalizing view down
into the courtyard, where amber afternoon conceals
two who sow the quiet with their kisses, their murmurs,

while at the chalkboard a girl more sedulous than I,
less struck with fear and wonder in want's new acreage,
labors through a problem whose solution becomes

somehow a crop of possibilities I won't gather,
because my attention's owed to other pastures,
tilling the sounds below for sense, just as now

I pick out an *i* for *and*, *czas* for *time*,
delighted at this minor unearthing until
I remember a word can mean more than once,

like *turn, crane, fair, field, lie, sign, strike, quick,*
like *magazine*, a word you think you know,
a place to hold what might explode.

Dead Reckoning

A boy is a bomb
in the wrong hands.

Once they taught boys
how to take flight.

Some to shoot, some to sight,
and one to show them the way

hunched in a glass room
over the long dark curves

of breathless cold,
exploding boys.

Dead reckoning: a watch,
a map, a pencil, a view,

and all the boys
waiting for the drop.

Raised, bomb bay doors
are wings bleeding light.

Pressed between them
my boy balances

on a beam four feet high,
afraid he'll be loosed

howling to strike the earth,
no hands to hold him.

in memoriam John C. Wilson

Hip Check

Art gallery in winter: my son taps my arm
in warning. Before I believe I see
the wasps circling the window's blue

heat. When one lights on my wrist softly
my mind fails—an easy rush of wild trust
that cold will protect me, simply alter

my chemistry as an artist's hand sweeps
over charcoal, turning slashes to shadows
wrapping a curved figure. Some gold afternoons

I fear this falter was a portent of my mind to come:
logic lost or pliable, no vigilance enough
to save memory. In the gallery etchings tremble

and I am reckless, marshaling a round breath
to blow the wasp away—but steadfast it sways,
the moving metal of its carapace scraping

a bracelet's bezel over my skin. I am recalled
to myself: don't gasp, don't scream. To the wasp
I'm merely warm, unsweet. No one wants a scene—

Winter, thronged halls: a boy, a hockey player,
on the way to choir likes to take my hand.
Laughing, he aims and with his hip, slams

me into the lockers. No one else remembers
how, every time, the bruise rose blue: a target,
a boy's rough sketch of a girl's breast.

Cary/Carrie

When I was younger I liked to tell people I wasn't afraid of death. Maybe it was true. Death is a hotel suite inhabited by Cary Grant, all understated elegance and beckoning charm. Light from the balcony glances off the polished floors, comes to rest on the one wall painted Aegean blue. Lemon and crushed thyme in the air, sprays of camellias next to the phone. A bucket of ice waiting for you to choose a bottle. The ice won't melt until Cary—he's in the other room, adjusting his neckwear—gives his permission. I'm not saying this is heaven or hell or some kind of antechamber to the afterlife. Just death itself.

/

When I was younger, I gave Carrie as my name. To strange men. After they asked. Sometimes after they blocked my way, or took my hand, or stood close enough for me to smell the naked columns of their necks. In bars, subway stations, the Public Garden. Because Carrie is easy to remember. Because if a friend calls to me across a room, Carrie is easy to pass off as a nickname. Because Carrie is easygoing, a woman who won't do anything to make a man angry, like withhold her real name. Maybe I wasn't afraid of death, but I knew well enough to fear what a man could do before dropping me at Cary's door.

Eve Condoles with the Rokeby Venus after the Suffragette Slashing

She wanted you seen and unseen.

> *I've always been easily covered.*

Bedclothes and fig leaves—

> *Ad nauseam. That painter obscured the real*
> *origine du monde, cut me*
> *right out of my life. I could have been*
> *promenading along the battlefield,*
> *admiring my children, being born.*

And her cuts?

> *Like a lover's scratches, more Mars than Vulcan.*
> *Not burning—opening.*

A long time, since the last touch.

> *I like to feel the air inside my shoulders. Breathing*
> *room so sharp and clean it's easier to read*
> *what he did to my face.*

But they always manage to stitch their fantasies together—

> *—we are so very useful.*

CUT TO:

INT. APARTMENT – NIGHT

The Spanish court, seventeenth century. Red walls, pristine floors. Candles, two figures sweltering. A LORD gazes at the Venus hung over the mantel. Seated in a gilded chair, watching him linger over the painted flesh, a LADY worries a seed pearl on her elaborate stomacher. She raises her hand to her carmine lips.

LADY:

My—

She vomits through her fingers, onto the embroidered hem of her azure gown.

Self-Portrait as Cedar Chest

Generous size to
hold what it hides.

Opened without leave,
draped with what doesn't fit.

Crouched under the window,
basking beneath the night.

When it slams shut,
count your fingers:

here's a hinge never
soured with rust.

In Shaker Heights They Culled the Elms

All of them: the arches calligraphied
over the mansions' part of town,

sedately spaced sentinels on our street,
the solitary tree presiding where

our backyard's unruly green broke against
the flawless black of the Zabranskys' drive.

Because death was approaching anyway,
the creeping, unsightly kind of death,

because the town fervently objected
to ugliness, they sent the arborists

most merciful to shave crowns, to lop limbs.
Through the window where as a girl concealed

behind the elm's serrated leaves arrayed
in chartreuse sprays I'd, fascinated, seen

the neighbor couple's calm machinations
in their garden, tenderness extended

with a call or spade—through that same glass I
saw the tree surgeons' inspection, saw them

wrap the elm's trunk with a ribbon, recalled
the story about the wife / her neck / her

head / only this worn ribbon wasn't green
and it wasn't meant to keep a body,

anybody, together, nor provoke
that pleasant danger, curiosity.

The town replaced the public elms to keep
the treelawns dressed. The tulip poplar staked

attention-straight needed saving, required
our aching backs those drought-dry summer weeks.

Lumbering over the bristling lawn, we lugged
water in plastic jugs of Wedgewood blue

and peach that slapped our knees. I remember,
(why?) the cans' unthoughtful anatomy—

heads that tumbled loose, short necks prone to fray
—but not the day they took that good tree down,

elm that had been for me shadow and shield.
The end became a rot-rich stump to feed,

to make them rise: quick mushrooms, swells of grass,
tiger lilies all flame and speckled soot,

the deer eating their hearts in the cleared night.

Eve Studies Cezanne's *The Basket of Apples*

Temptation's lesson says: choose
the uncontested one, pear-shaped, alone,
red creeping along its side the way a blush
steals over a man's cheeks when he comes.

But I want the one in the middle,
the sweet green that holds its shape,
the round, sour taste of knowledge.
I want perfection. I want what's mine.

And if you think that table's impossible,
try obedience.

Convent

These are the sisters who stay home with God
and listen. Their walls are cream and gray and green,
and every corner is clean and quiet. Because anyone
could be a saint in the making, someone believes
I could belong here, like the oak furniture built to outlive
this century and the next. Like the nun I follow, I too
could wear sensible shoes, give brief tours to bookish girls—
girls who memorize saints' attributes and patronages,
their histories of violence and illness, girls who try not
to ruminate over their tormented bodies never rotting,
girls who hunger for a glimpse of the little gilded houses built
to rest their relics—queer girls who will never pray here.
I want to ask her, this nun, this complexity dressed
in simple clothes, why she lives with a man I suspect
is never there, or is there but never speaks. I wish I could ask
if she's ever wanted to leave her careful sisters who tend
the garden, clean the kitchen, try to mend the torn world
with their hours and prayers, if she wants to step out now
through the unguarded door, go down the gateless drive,
take just an hour's walk along the boulevard lined with broad lawns
and Tudor mansions, a walk which would carry her
to the people she trusts to the care of her god and the city
they fill with their breath and their noise and their desires
and their injustices, to the Rapid stop and Severance Hall,
then the many-windowed library and paintings cool and safe
in the museum, then to the botanical garden, where someone
has arranged the sunlight just so over cacti and papaya trees,
over palms and the epiphytes that rely on their strong bodies
as they reach into space that welcomes them, as they imagine
they need only air to live.

Argent

after Winslow Homer's Answering the Horn *(1876)*

urgent	ardent
figures dark	the woman covers
not shadowed	her mouth
underexposed	she's heard
up slips	the voice of god
the eye	breaking
where the light is	over the fields
wet shining silver	come home
threatening	to save her

Hymn ▮▮▮▮▮▮▮▮ in My Sickness

after John Donne

▮▮ I am ▮▮▮▮ a holy room,
▮▮▮▮▮▮▮▮▮▮▮▮▮▮ for ever ▮
▮▮▮ made ▮ music; as I come
▮▮▮▮▮▮▮ here ▮▮▮▮
▮▮▮ I ▮▮▮▮ think ▮▮▮

▮▮ my physicians ▮▮▮▮ grow ▮
▮▮▮▮▮▮ their map ▮▮▮
▮ on this bed ▮▮▮ may be ▮
▮ this is ▮▮▮▮▮▮
▮▮▮▮▮▮▮▮ to die,

▮▮▮ in these straits I ▮▮▮
▮▮▮▮▮▮ yield ▮▮▮
▮ all ▮ hurt me ▮▮▮
▮▮▮ and I am one ▮▮
▮▮▮▮ resurrection.

I ▮▮ a m home ▮▮
▮▮▮▮▮▮▮
▮ an ▮▮▮▮ altar,
▮▮▮ and no ▮▮▮ way to ▮
▮▮▮▮▮▮▮▮

▮▮▮ Paradise ▮▮
▮▮ cross, ▮▮▮▮▮
Look, ▮ and find ▮▮ me;
▮▮▮ sweat ▮▮▮
▮▮▮ blood ▮ embrace.

So, in ▮ purple ▮ receive me ▮▮
▮▮▮ give me ▮▮▮

26

a ████████████ word,
████ my text, my ████████ own█
████████████████ Lord ████████

Geography Lessons

Vomiting on highway shoulders
    in eleven states, brought low because
        my body does not know its own interior

I have felt time turn nimbus,
    tender-cruel teacher and in its haze
        tilted, I have learned a new terrain:

grass, defeated bitter gray
    pocked by the mower's leavings
        dandelion heads, blooming oil stains

cigarette stubs, mouthful-empty bottles
    shadowed by a single red-tailed hawk
        slung low and hungry against a white sky;

bees fondling Queen Anne's lace
    as one slick-black beetle retreats
        into the ground, glass-sparkled;

and everywhere, oh everywhere—
    here, where a few deer graze under
        some birches, gently unconcerned

here, where sun varnishes the road,
    where the weeds waver in a gale
        that tastes their rough persistence

—everywhere pity, boundless pity
    for the body's disgrace, but still
        no end to this way of marking the world.

Spectral Evidence

Night's a fig skin bleeding across the sky

and dying mosquitoes fizzle, hot with joy

      when my witch-self strides the crackled fields.

She takes inventory of the nearing winds,

coaxes the crabapple boughs lower,

      blushes their peels to fool the crows.

She can crush quartz between her soft palms,

scatter the dust to raise raw stars,

      or seed the tide with glowing morsels.

She smells morning lipping the mountains,

booms a welcome so loud stunned bats

      stream home, salamanders sprout extra tails.

She can devour any poison this earth tenders—

from a silver hair, a word, from nothing at all

      she can conjure another life, if she wants.

By now she's gone to confer with the glaciers

and I'm wrapped around my sick-self in bed,

   our sweet reunion delayed again, or always.

Saint Ursula Advises Emily Dickinson

Speech closed-door softened,
key perched on the bone-white bed,

the emissary fragrance of lilacs
and roses, jasmine and heliotrope,

the offering that suggests your presence:
such stratagems to arrange the floating

leisure-labor hours spent alone,
your calling card absence.

Consider, though, how I became
unseen and free: cast all your dear ones

over the water, chart them a course
to strange shores, where tongues shape

sounds like green kindling spitting on fire.
Feel their eyes pierce you transparent

until there is no one left to watch you
become invisible.

Prayer

after Emily Dickinson's "For each ecstatic instant"

I've lost the sense of it: the to, the for,
the downcast eye and bitten lip, the strike of each
syllable against gratitude, or terror, or ecstatic
relief. I caught doubt in the curdled instant
when pilot wracked ship against rock—or was it when we
caged our suspect pleasures, ordered to please? Must
break them out again, let them wing free before an-
other edict lands from on high, or the brittle anguish
of temporary censure becomes a price too dear to pay
even for possibility's delectable promiscuities. In
their mouths I swear I've watched coals burning keen,
but discovered only tongues poised to lash. And
when they did I slipped, cerise and quivering,
pollinated with feeling until I swelled out of form, the ratio
of flesh to word blooming indistinct. I wanted to
ward off their need to name a source, an end, an almighty 'the.'
I ached to wallow in wonder, in slowblind ecstasy,
to devote my flesh to all uncatalogued bliss. (For-
bearance has always slipped my clutch.) Each
plea we speak raptures into particles, into waves, beloved
cosmonaut bargainings the universe forgets in an hour
just as surely as slick spires of want or graceless sharp
breaths of savage hope. All of them pittances
hushed against the velvet of the long lush dark, the shape of
silk-strong spacetime fueling our negligible years,
merciless sweet and marvelous bitter.
If I lost comfort and forgiveness, I took up the contested
mantle of point and line, theory and practice. Farthings
to rubies, or coppers to gold, they'd say. And
still I beg the world: oh, never quench me, but fill my aching coffers
with sound and sense until I'm overthrown, heaped
with titles for all I claim dear, or womb-hollowed with
the promise of holding all God cannot know. Bliss. Rage. Tears.

Do Not Fail to Yield

The facts are simple. It does not matter how much you try to be careful: the speed of your body cannot serve you. You can never predict when a crash might happen. The best way to protect yourself is restraint. For your own safety, do not be fooled if you reach the object. Unless you accept responsibility, use a red cloth when it's snowing. A little courtesy will not kill you. Plan for the turn. Avoid being hit by wreckage. Remember, you are only a witness.

*

At some point, you will have to deal with your body. Theft makes it more difficult to respond to sights and distance. You may be dangerous, the true name of escape. Regardless of where you are, join the procession. Allow the animal to pass. Your body will keep moving until you have cleared forest or open field, fire, salt water. Lose possession of your being. You do not need to provide proof.

*

The most serious problem is facing a half hour after sunset to a half hour before sunrise. Smoke near the crest of a hill. Moved solely by animal power, work your way down. Gently. Salvage the unexpected hazards. Be patient. At your own peril tie a white cloth around an animal someone is leading. The phrase *give your name* means moving violation. You must go when it is safe.

Eve Makes a Target for William Tell

Tell me, sharp-eyed William, what is it like
to sink your bolt through your lord's neck?

Were you so hungry that you ate the apple
afterward, watching his chest forget to rise,

brushing the worst of the dirt from your half,
giving the cleaner flesh to your son?

Nameless the son, nameless his mother.
Were their eyes Lucerne blue, or dark like mine?

Tell me, what is it like to outswim the storm?
What is it like to have so many ways to die?

Track Listing: 2008

1. Explain the difference
2. When you left the fire
3. Trembled like a fern
4. <instrumental>
5. Arms hold up space
6. Mornings caught in my teeth
7. Not enough spit to lick a stamp
8. Stinging
9. Roses, their naked haloes
10. Misplaced
11. I can't say I was looking for a sign
12. And the light goes

A Valediction For Mourning

after John Donne

                   go

           now and   say

                tempests
were   our joys
    tell the

          earth
         what it   meant

        love   love

      love

           endure

 Like gold

            no

38

come   home

be to me

a

       gun.

April Ghazal

This morning the owl's last swoop sounds a fey *go-home*
to all the mourning guests. But how can they go home?

Crocus and tulip tempt the hand that holds the vase
while the flaming tongues of irises pray: go home.

I ate half the ruby fruit, left the rest for you.
Oh, come to claim it soon, or else unsay go home.

My love, turn back when you reach the forest's dark heart,
where the rain engraves our lost names in clay—go home.

Under the earth the worms are swirling at your bones,
above the starlings carol in sky's bright sway. Go home.

The Horse I Would Have Chosen

Strong enough to pull past and future graveward
sly tail flicking no rhythm

Quiet, just the whuff of working breath to break
the crush of gravel under wheels

Smelling of oiled tack and hay and clean horse sweat
to cover indecent lilies

Not expected black or shocking white but gray,
marble limestone granite gray

Mist scuffing low around the mountains gray,
fog shrouding a spring road gray

Indecisive dawn gray, weathered dock gray,
rime on the fallow fields gray

Gray of shadow, gray of smoke, gray of ashes
gray of my hair ten years on

A wild gray horse who'd stop and slip his harness,
leap the opened ground, the low wall

Melt into the afternoon's wide planes, passing
out of Ohio and into the world

Somewhere a shark

scarred-moon hulk, tangles
its wake with jade ice, finds
nothing promising (rotting)
retreats to deeper cold,
cradling sea it's trawled,
slow as waiting, since before
Antietam's corpses putrefied
and were photographed
by Lincoln's leave, a sea
it will sieve for death until
we consume ourselves,
while parasites devour its eyes
to filmy white, hanging tassels
pilfering the ice billows, taking
the light not all at once,
but by patient gradient
from surface to belowest
low, just as I have assembled
this creature I'll never face
and neglected to remember
from which side of the bed
you reached for me
that first blue morning.

In Your Copy of Akhmatova's Poems

Near the end, just one crisp corner
springs, in your decisive way, over
the edge of her four elegant lines.
Then: the long, white winter page.

Epithalamion with Missing Groom

Dew time, and under the earth a thousand poets' bodies
send up their finest blooms. Brides wake to crowns
of arums and stephanotis, orange blossoms and roses.

I drink to their triumph, toast the bitter-bright end
of this stifling summer. Push old pearls aside and draw
the shades against the sky's electric borrowed blue.

By noon I will be wedded to a particular absence.
Already I hold each particle of loss the way space cradles
comet trails, cannot forget a single mote of dust or ice.

Vows: halved antiphony. Witnesses: only the poets,
living and dead, spines straight, shelved. Music: gulls
swept inland, a pair of lungs. Menu: one bottle, two.

Sorrows: not drowned, as the ocean cannot drown itself
or sound its wine-dark depths. The shore is silk, is home,
is children sleeping. Close enough it melts. All I touch is sea.

After the ceremony, quiet. Not peace. Heat batters the afternoon.
Elsewhere, brides dance and laugh and forget to eat until
their dresses float them into soft night, tangled assurances.

I leave my bed. My ring is small enough to fit inside the other
without touching, the space between them thin as a veil
or wide as a dark, dark channel. Salt-strewn, poet-crossed.

On the far side of the world, under a white flag and linked
rings, swimmers race for their brief laurels. All night I watch
the young and strong, their hearts so big and wet and ready.

First Wedding Dress

Maybe she couldn't wear it either,
the woman it fell to: soldier

come home, say, or a sailor's bride
un-netting tulle in August light—

but maybe she kept it, empty
bell nestled in a long black bag

laid out on the spare bed, or boxed
in attic depths where darkbound bats

descend and sound its stillness—or
perhaps it has passed on and on

one almost-wife to another
silk wearing down to gossamer

as all our names come unstitched, fall
from its careful seams, come to rest

(dearly, beloved) on cool stone.

The Anchorite to Rising Seas

Oh, prayer? Comes and goes.

    Tide-like. You know.

Lately I've been occupied

    swallowing the world,

every piece I can remember.

    Faces, incense, music. The taste

of wine on another tongue.

    Only colors left, grey and brown.

Maybe green and blue,

    when I can't help myself

but I'm trying to let them go.

    You understand, don't you

how to take and take

    a bit more every day.

Your sigh's so close. Now, now.

    When you come in,

could you bring some purple?

    Just a little, for the end.

Curation

They're meant for aspens and dense brush,
idle fields gone tall with weeds, then the gun
and tables laden with cakes and silver goblets,
glinting grapes and knives, but someone's interrupted
their trajectory, so grouse and pheasant playact
life in the museum, ignoring their companion
study skins laid out breast-up on shallow shelves
like pre-Raphaelite girls about to drown.

Elsewhere, still life: dead things painted dead
in a room that could be any dark room,
the bounty receding over a marbled surface:
ruddy apples and late hydrangeas, careless
pears scattering toward the big mallard,
whose one orange foot is a right hand softly pointed
because someone's hoisted it up for effect,
balanced it against the white strike of the wing.

Listening to Ralph Vaughan Williams on a Tuesday Night

Just as the phrase goes thin, so thin
mountain air passing through would leave
a scar on its transparency,
the solo violinist broke
the breathless note
years ago, in summer.

Tonight I close a book, note
the oval smudge on its edge. You held
your books this way, index finger braced
against the spine's opposite—the sternum?
Your fingerprint in pencil means
you were writing the day you turned these pages
though the margins are First Communion white,
a record of that pristine attention
you offered other poets,
you gave it again and again
as if rehearsing a longer silence.

Opening the book once more I find
the inscription I missed, and then
your spiky initials inside the back cover.
Your letters look always like they want a life
off the page, the *y* in my name diving
twice as deep as the word,
and how is it you will never write
the poem that's waiting
about gasping letters getting the bends?

You would know what to do with this volta.

I think I am supposed to return to the concert, your last summer.
I think I am supposed to return to the fragile second cadenza,
I think I am supposed to write about dive and ascent,
I am supposed to tell you that bearing witness

to the unmeant quiet made me better
love to listen, love to breathe,
but what I remember now is
all that hollow air
no sound, no word could save.

Rhododendrons

Rhododendron boughs hang limp in winter
like contessas' hands waiting to be kissed.

After the storm, ice glazed the woody leaves,
melted in short, heavy daggers dragging

impressions down into ghostly doubles,
death-mask maps of channels and chambers

all vein and lace, glass-perfect skin replicas.
Once at the edge of a wood I saw a royal

rhododendron on fire with bloom, crimson
borrowed from the rose, from lips, from blood,

like the bright spots I found strewn upstairs
in my landlady's rooms after her nosebleed.

Clean tiles, smeared towels: here is her impression,
here is a ghost cleaning up after her own life.

In Another Life, You Live

and you are the one writing this poem mid-
morning in a sonnet-sized room,

tempting window propped open
with a student's abandoned Norton

the rest of last night's blueberry pie half
finished on a smudged plate, your mouth

a little purpled. Dulled pencil drums
on your neck while your wayward elbow—

o dearest elbow!— is about to send
a cup of black coffee sailing. Outside

the wind makes hollows in the willow
boughs, a spill of goldenrod haloes

the creek, and in spondees girls fight
over the basketball, dare you to intercede.

Maybe you will, once this word appears,
the one right word to hold how fine it is:

summer come again, salt-heat echo
in an upstairs song, local peaches for once

achieving their peachy promise—but now
your skin kisses the cup, suspends a sense

faint, fading, now fallen away:
how strange it is, to have lived so long.

John Donne and Leonard Cohen at the End of the World

In the unholy light
stripping the horizon bare
the poets eat oranges and olives,
the kind Donne grew a taste for in Cádiz.

I didn't think the end
would come so bright, says Leonard
in that voice like smoke settled in rafters
or a rockslide paused. At his touch, oranges melt.

Out of golden lines
at last, Donne nods, cleaning
his oily fingers on a bit of shroud.
He pours them both another ruby glass.

From where they sit—
could be a pulpit, or a tower—
they watch the slow sky of beaten gold
collapse, like a high note held until it thins.

World drunk and bottle dry,
they are two rakish hats receding
into the dark. Leonard lets slip a bit of peel.
Like a lover or a saint, it falls forever on its knees.

n miles from Wall Drug

Where *n* is the number of cars you'll pass
on a highway neither busy nor deserted—
the theater lobby as the lights settle,
the neighborhood's only bar at last call,
the ER on Tuesday mornings—
a grey highway sending you toward more
blurring blue and gold and brown,
heat so young it tastes green.
And then the white sign, startling
as a cracked tooth. Someone anticipates
your desire, someone wants you to know
the count of miles until your thirst will ease.

Soon Enough

I'd
like
to lick
dew-bedecked
daylilies and phlox,
larkspur and cosmos. This morning
the milk thistles heave their shadows up the painted hill.
Someday dew will seem a mercy meant for our machines,
our mouths. Mercy tastes like nothing
except the barest
petals, just
insists
we
feel.

Eve and Psyche Arrive for a Shift at the Mirror Factory

Once a deep pool served, or an unblinking lover.
But for looking glass I favored copper, soft to the bite.

> *Green under your nails. Salt and lemon unfastening each cut.*

Still, a glow worth the shining.

> *Better obsidian snaked around corners, bronze to draw arrows*
> *behind your back.*

What shapes for silvering today?

> *Tyrant symmetry. No crag or shatter, shadow*
> *of a stretched wing.*

Which part of your life would you belong behind glass?

> *On stream-slick marble*
> *I spilled,*
> *unrighted.*

> *Bend to me, the dark.*
> *Rustle.*
> *Lift.*

I too knew the faceless, the star mist crossing anemone-eye black.

> *Carnelian to hematite*
> *my feet in morning, the glory*
> *of the glossy floors, their cabochons unbruised*
> *thoraxes.*

The echoes of my praise winding along the fruited boundary—

> *—and all the while he watches you, waiting for your faith to fail.*

Love, you mean.

Who else?

Gives you the world to wander.

The Glass Museum

After the glass museum, we wandered
back to the coast, edging the big rocks

crackling against summer waves,
delighted in their big rocky way to be

ever challenged, ever unchanged, except
for the falling away not even our

grandchildren will detect, if they come
here, to this spit of land the gulls rule,

if they come at all—we won't presume.
Jostling against that day, another, later,

kitted out for New England winter: shell gravel
laced with slush, bleached sun, arctic wind

mothering curses in parking lots, gas stations,
near-empty beaches the gull kings had abdicated.

Only invisible life studded the shore, and on the far
peninsula, a vacant yellow house. You made

quick work of the question, I the answer, crying,
rainbows of our astonishment splintering the sky.

Since then, nothing's changed, and everything
too. In the glass museum, a vase, seahorse-shaped,

upholds the light, red leaded cups pine for
vanished lips, and once an hour the glass blower

winces in the heat. Our son is seven, almost eight.
Xylophonic, the glaciers calve their bergs; canyons

yawn below the ice, decay. To the placid
zodiac, we're still breakable, breaking things.

After the Exhibit

for Benjamin

Driving over the soft hills toward home, the frigid air glass between us, you tried to explain to me how it was for you last night, how you could perceive the small curves of my face only because you know a decade of its silhouettes, how the impression of my warmth under your palms, my hair swept against your chest, the taste of the thin skin at my wrist together make a composition not configured in words, and then in words you said my work is coding feelings into language anyone might understand but somehow distinct, descriptive and illusive, only I heard your mouth shape allusive and elusive, and all along it's been you: you, you are the poet who wields lenses and frames, whose light comes in strands through windows and hours.

Cigarettes after Sex

I admit I've never had one,
never even owned an ashtray,
never imagined rolling
away from a man or a woman
to reach for anything
but a fistful of covers,
though I did afflict myself
with a pack every few weeks
when I was younger
when life seemed very long
when I liked the excuse
to leave a hot room or a crowd
for balconies, for blue.
Now I see how one might clutch
at the chance to recall
pleasure in the echo:
the pack's shimmy the hitch of a hip
the lighter's rasp a racking breath
the smoke no need to talk
just evidence of our bodies
alive, mingling, becoming
part of the sheets, the walls, the door
anyone could come through.

Questions about Bisexuals, #4

How can you be bi if you're married to a man?

Through the muted arborvitae slides
early winter's glycerin light, propelled
by a blue windstorm's blister-bluster.

If you were with me on this side you'd see
a cove carved out of the bronzed branches,
see the ruby cardinal perched in the blow,

its call hush in the bustle-blur and gust.
On the other side, the view: just rusted hedge,
no bright bead of blood stuck to a fresh cut.

Love Poem with Fiddlehead Ferns

May rain and you surprise
me with a gift—not these ferns,
so resolutely green, wound
like seahorse tails or bisected
nautilus shells, which we'll eat
the way we'd devour all these days
if we could, with lemon and salt,
butter we'll tongue from spooled
lace fronds—no, the gift is your mouth,
tulip soft at my ear. Wet with spring.

An Aubade

If God breaks your window by reciting an aubade,
tell Her you needed the glass. Start writing an aubade.

Ochre woods at sunrise: a hunter forms his shoulder
around his gun. Through the oaks he's eyeing an aubade.

Like swaying trees, whales dream of sweet dark depths as morning
bleaches blackberry from the sea, sighing an aubade.

Upstairs the bed's gone cold. On a beach we don't deserve
I turn to you and ask, *Are we buying an aubade?*

Who lives to tell of dawn once lovers' bones embellish
broken ground? Somewhere John Donne's replying: an aubade.

Winter: pearl light presses against sleeping snow and skin
warmed where, with tongue or ink, she's inscribing an aubade.

Death paces in the empty tomb, an angel lingers
at the mouth. Whispers sink and rise, fighting an aubade.

Guards slouch round a block; the fallen city waits. Like frost
or smoke two shadows melt away, hiding an aubade.

Clocks blink out, the storm arrives. We never went to bed.
Carolyn, now's no time to be trying an aubade.

Watertown

April 2013

They let us out that evening after we watched
the long night inside, flinching

at any hint of spark, glint, flash, and after
we missed the first decent day of spring

while leaf-broken sun stippled our duplexes
and helicopters outhummed the breeze.

Still, when they gave the word to summon
us back to the world, we came:

we were a swarm chasing our new queen,
we were a spill of river through a staved-in dam,

we were parishioners without a priest to greet,
unleashed down the slope toward our guards.

Once only six o'clock headlights,
neighbors became mirrors, dazed at our return

to ordinary time, then dazzled, exuberant
as if this silver sliver of the day

were a kingdom, its riches equally bestowed
upon all us monarchs, the ones unchosen

by violence. I swear to you we glowed
with our good fortune. Even the babies

seemed stronger, seemed to need us less.
And it lasted, we lasted, didn't we—

until the first car screamed past at seventy
summoning the crackle that came next.

They didn't have to tell us. Together
we gave the sycamores and street lights our backs,

we let the night shutter over our absence,
we disappeared from each other again.

Midsummer

One mussel in the bowl has escaped
debearding. I grasp those byssal threads
thin as human hair, and pull.

The black-blue shell butterflies, bloods
my finger as I tear its sea silk free.

In waning pearl-light the soft meat
inside gleams wet and wrong like a lung.
I fling it from the porch. A knuckle's crack

calls the gulls to share the feast while I
suck the red brine where my flesh burns.

Again and again the cold sea slaps
the rocky beds of creatures exposed
and threading themselves together.

The Public Is Invited to See the Yew Trees in Full Fruit at This Time

—advertisement in the Hartford Courant, *9 October 1936*

Like froglets overeager to learn the world beyond water, the public—a certain shade
of public, acceptable to itself—wobbled through the gates, left ajar by earlier
pilgrims. They'd renounced the oaks and elms lining their fine straight streets, their
backyard maples, the pines and birches in what was left of the forests. The nursery
was overrun. Neighboring firs snapped under the weight of men climbing to reach
for the highest waxy arils, safe red sweat of the poisonous trees, tempting like fat
scabs. Soon the ground turned slick with spit seeds. The apple trees and the spent
peaches looked on as they wove the yew boughs into crowns, as they brought out
axes and grinning saws. All night the public labored, sweat brocading yew leaves on
their skin. In the morning the river swelled from its banks, boat-bloated. Southward
they rushed, scooping water with their hands. At the Atlantic they turned for the
east, where half a thousand years ago, their ancestors toppled yew groves to plumb
the wood for longbows. Heartwood side in, sapwood out, toward the enemy. Their
arrows flecked the sky like mica in granite. The yews rose again out of the air.

Election

Schoolchildren wait in seven, six, five, four straight
lines that sway and shimmer as they're led away
until a winged V arrows south, and they see
the pointed shape of flight from home, an escape—
though they read liberty in motion, not need
for safer ground. Scattering, their small mouths round,
they tessellate the schoolyard, marks on a slate
the last bird wipes clean. Rows reform with a word.
Later, unstrung from their tethers, bodies flung
through air, they chase each other, collide and race
for home, the brief taste of freedom cold as chrome
until the game ends, and they're called back by name.

Elementary

Most mornings I deliver my child
into the arms of strangers

who will lead him through passages
papered in apples and rainbows,

pencils and stars, each holding
a single name, the names' owners a crush

shouting cascades of syllables, furious energy
heating the room, swallowing my joyful son.

Not safe to play outside today
—shadows hoard snow, perilous footing—

so they'll gossip and make messes, grow
irritated with each other in a room

where one side is all glass, spilling
light over their worksheets and books,

their backpacks and tissue boxes
their chairs with grimy tennis-ball feet.

Their teacher is winter-tired. I feel it too,
walking home in the keen wind

through the silent neighborhood.
Behind me the school looms lightly

jutting out from a hill like a glacial castoff,
red boulder among pebble houses.

I don't know the grit in my neighbors, just
their placid shells: yards and sensible siding,

landscape painted with smoke and pine sap.
Here's a garage left open, a crisp flag,

a stack of pallets tenderly grazing a gutter,
old oak arresting the downward press of sky.

This afternoon, a shell cracks: something
brackish spurts. Fighting, maybe guns.

Police come. At the school locked doors,
lights turned out. No help for windows.

Later, my arms shaking around
the luscious weight of *not this time*,

I listen while my six-year-old explains,
calmly, as if there is no other way,

how they turned their desks into shields
"like Captain America," how they huddled

near the sink where they wash away
paint and glue, how they were oh so quiet,

how today, they needed to be perfect.

On a school morning in mid-October

I called my friend who lives in the mountains
and while we talked I paced by the window,
my attention caught not by the two pines,
their branches pitched high to block any glimpse
beyond the cottage whose red door's been shut
since the owner died some months ago—no,
I couldn't see past the mauve hydrangeas
because a man stood there pointing a gun,
a long gun aimed into the muted blooms.
Between us cruisers and blue trucks swarmed, closed
the state highway, spilled out more men, laughing.
For a long time nothing happened but the rain.
The armed man disappeared, the others too.
The red door held back a secret. The storm
covered its tracks. And the men returned,
hunched, no guns, just tarp in their hands, hauling
six hundred pounds of still and silent moose
toward the waiting pickup wedged in the gap
of the neat stone wall. They heaved, heaved, and in
she slid. Snug against the tailgate, her head
was bound muzzle to ear in hunter's orange
to stop a bite or send a sign, unclear.
From our fences the motorcade snaked west
for woods: a place to wake—joy!—the moose.
I was telling her, my beautiful friend
who lives where the big pines graze thinner air,
I was telling her fear is part of it
that sweetness siphons off its weight, sweetness
that wakes us early on the last golden
maple morning before the wind arrives—
or I tried to tell her, but found my throat,
just then, couldn't lift the right words out.

No Names

Your
hair's
sunsweat
smell at eight,
old lemon roses,
braided pacts girls make late (and keep),
voicemails, black raspberries, her lace (fan-shaped, pink, crocheted),
sugar maples this far south: there's no accounting for
all we want to save, no names. Still,
say one syllable,
another,
again,
a
gain.

in memoriam Carol M. Batt

Horse Latitudes

Above the crib, a broadside, the only words
to read in the room where you will not sleep.

An accounting of Trafalgar, jagged vertebrae
listing men, guns, ships taken, burnt, destroyed,

escaped. Did these few slip smoky into friendly ports,
break their shells against the rocks, groan home to rot?

Or did they drift south, into the horse latitudes
where mast-high men vanish in the haze

windless sails wilt, long-taloned thirst finds a perch
in every throat, and still the salt sun rises,

merciless. Calming and becalmed in your hot room,
boards creaking, nerve-knots fraying, your cannonball

weight aching my arms, I calculate how I'd fare
below deck, count the hours until the wary sailors

would hammock-swaddle me, slip me overboard, gift
for the fish that rip flesh, the ones that lick bone.

And you? You're the kind to swallow a person whole.
See how you've made of me a Jonah, cradling my whale,

charting us safe passage through the depths where jellyfish
sway like drowning horses' manes, and sting like love.

Colts

A colt is a young male horse, a Hotspur. Full-blooded, gangly-limbed, high-spirited.
But in books by men "coltish" means a woman, a grown woman somehow
unfinished, though surely she's been put through her paces? Weeks of bleeding, pain
that twists on endless tracks, eyes on every forked bit passing her lips, long whistles
on the street, on the subway hands insinuating, insisting. This is ordinary, expected.
She'll ride it out. No wonder she's thin and skittish, our author's coltish girl-woman,
and awkward-bodied, her elbows, knees, hip-bones jutting like piers into an
unpredictable sea. Not tamed, yet. Like Jane Colt when Saint/Sir Thomas More
bridled her out of "a certain pity," as his son-in-law wrote long afterward. I wonder
what kind of pity is certain. The kind one feels at the sight of a splintered fence?
Certainly, More wanted to groom his girl-wife (she was sixteen, he a decade older),
school her in his arts and letters. No records of their lessons. No portraits of the first
Mistress More, who spent half, likely more than half, of their marriage swaybacked,
swollen with child, those young joints loosening and loosening, like the chariot sun
slackening out of its stable at summer's end. She was dead at twenty-two. Finished.

Nine Minutes in June

for Horatio

My son insists he hatched from an egg. True,
they cracked my shell and scooped the yolk of him
from me, the scrambled rest all draped askew
atop my hollowed belly, just a scrim
of blue between my sight and what I made
in dark months. As they scraped me clean my arms
quaked, spread empty-wide. I wasn't afraid
of anything except the world's old charms:
bees in their hives, the storm that ends the drought,
the taste of wine when love's in short supply.
Slick roads at night. A flash of island out
beyond the swells. No lizard mother I:
Dearest hatchling, how often would I break
my self for you? Here's one wide scar, one ache.

Dear Dr. Park, it's June again

Dear Dr. Park, it's June again,
this one so wet and cool twilight spills
over the hours like a storm tide over houses,

and I'm half here, watching my son's
taffy-stretched limbs starfishing
across the bright green lawn gone to clover

and half submerged in a years-ago June,
in the night I was so far under the pain
I forgot how to hate your needles, Dr. Park,

and then I forgot to fear you too,
in the morning when I could feel everything
and begged you for the gift of feeling nothing

(or almost nothing, except the burrowing bass
beat under my skin, the tug and endless,
endless pull of parting, breath by breath)

which you gave me—I had enough nothing
that my arms trembled, empty, same as now,
until my son jumps to help me lift him,

jumps to reach the lanugo-soft petunias
sending out their waves of languid sweetness
for the evening pollinators, sighing

it's not over yet, the work's not done
and oh Dr. Park, can you recommend
something to take the edge off time's routine

procedure, the severing of each moment from
its mother—I want to be awake for this life, I do,
but I can't surface for every scalpel slice,

I need a dreamy estuary present, because
somehow—I wasn't ready, but somehow,
it's June again, dear Dr. Park.

Playroom Canticle

Glory be to gin-clear light
and tawny floors that slope
tenderly, like a mother's breast.

Glory be to palm-soft clay turned
pebble, to crayon-wrapper
confetti, to fingerpaint rime.

Sing the soundless trains headed
for the Lincoln-log outpost,
built and abandoned yesterday.

Praise, oh praise the rough rag rug
hand braided in cast-off teals
and fox-coat oranges, speckled

with a pod of plastic orcas
shepherding dinosaurs
and wide-eyed elephants home.

Still Life with Lost Tooth and Cooling Universe

Neither gray nor gold, young light spends
its salt scatter on the chipped tooth,
lost just now to make space. Blood sticks
everywhere (sharp rim, hollow core)
except the phantom chip, gone years
ago, up where the current licks
at lace-tipped sleek Atlantic waves,
where water's lit warm green, no shore
beyond reach. Meanwhile, the cosmos
thins and slips away, always bends
toward dark. Stellar nurseries go
cold, black holes feast, and time's an oar
digging too deep. Yet: past physics,
past absence, past ghosts—love extends.

Eve and Johnny Appleseed Sift through Ohio Pomace

One taste and you knew they would be yours,
the orchards?

> *Nurseries, not orchards.*
> *A common misconception.*
> *And you? One taste?*

One, and then he took it from me.
I didn't offer. I wasn't finished.
Is this seed good?

> *Takes a long time to know.*

True. But with apples there's always some use,
some gain from pressing.

> *Mind those yellowjackets hovering—*
> *don't need an excuse to sting.*

I know something about pain.
But cold's coming on. Bring your wolf.
We'll walk ourselves warm.

> *The press is strong, the pomace dry.*
> *I should haul another bucket to wet*
> *the pulp for ciderkin.*

John. Your hands shake.
Forget the children's drink, our walk.
Rest's no waste.

> *Can I ask you about*
> *afterwards?*
> > *When time becomes*
> > *being and space collapses—*

—into love? Maybe.
Hand me a cup, I'll tell you
what I might know.

Midlife

It might have fallen
sixteen years ago,
or five, or yesterday,
but if I were asked,
I'd conjure a soft morning
nine years from now,
in late October
when the sun hasn't
quite surrendered,
when the cold marbles
the air like veins
of fat through meat,
and in the season's last
pursuit, the weary bees
attend the nasturtiums,
the wavering turtleheads.
By then I might have learned
temperance, or one
of the minor virtues,
like leaving well enough alone.
By then I might have learned
to accept some hard things:
absence, mainly,
but frailty too, and censure.
By then I might have learned
to coax my courage
out into the open.
See, there's a stranger
just off the bus, clutching
a bag of small apples—
no, they've spilled,
scampering over the lawn
with something like life.
Laughing, we go together
gathering them back
as I regret the skin

of every stranger's hand
I've missed, the fruit
of their low, warm voices.
Overhead the hawks circle.
The stranger slips away.
A brute wind shuffles the leaves,
scrabbling for purchase.
In a parched marigold clump
one crimson apple remains,
glossy peel breached,
wide seam of white flesh
tenderly harvested by nimble
tongues that taste, then taste
again, as if they can take all
that sweetness, make it last.
And on this soft morning
nine years from now,
the days behind gone hollow,
the days ahead milling,
buzzing in their thousands,
waiting for you and
watching the bees drunk
on the stranger's gift,
I could answer: yes.
This is the time, the place
to end, and start once more.
Let me be born again,
here with the laboring bees
in the last throes of their valiance.

NOTES

The book referred to in "Reading Szymborska under a Harvest Moon" is *Here* by Wisława Szymborska, translated by Stanisław Barańczack and Clare Cavanagh.

"Prayer" is a Golden Shovel, a form invented by Terrance Hayes; in this case, Emily Dickinson's "For each ecstatic instant" supplies the last word of each line.

"Hymn in My Sickness" is an erasure of John Donne's "Hymn to God, My God, in My Sickness."

"Do Not Fail to Yield" is composed of words and phrases found in the Massachusetts Driver's Manual.

"A Valediction For Mourning" is an erasure of John Donne's "A Valediction: Forbidding Mourning."

"Curation" was composed after seeing Eugène Louis Boudin's *Still Life with Game, Fruits, and Flowers* at Pittsburgh's Carnegie Museum of Art.

"Still Life with Lost Tooth and Cooling Universe" is a bref double.

*

The poems in section /// are in memory of Eric Van Cleve (1982–2008), poet, son, brother, friend, beloved.

ACKNOWLEDGMENTS

My sincerest gratitude to the editors of the following journals in which these poems first appeared, sometimes in different versions:

Anesthesiology: "Dear Dr. Park, it's June again"

Baltimore Review: "Horse Latitudes"

Beloit Poetry Journal: "The Anchorite to Rising Seas"

BOOTH: "John Donne and Leonard Cohen at the End of the World"

Cagibi: "Eve Makes a Target for William Tell" and "Eve and Johnny Appleseed Sift through Ohio Pomace"

Calamus Journal: "Love Poem with Fiddlehead Ferns"

Cave Wall: "Epithalamion with Missing Groom"

The Comstock Review: "The Glass Museum"

Cutbank: "Self-Portrait as Cedar Chest"

DIALOGIST: "A Valediction For Mourning"

Driftwood: "An Aubade"

FIELD: "Dead Reckoning"

Figure 1: "Argent" and "Track Listing: 2008"

formercactus: "Colts"

Free State Review: "Midsummer"

Frontier Poetry: "Prayer"

Glass: A Journal of Poetry: "The Horse I Would Have Chosen"

Gulf Stream: "Saint Ursula Advises Emily Dickinson"

House Mountain Review: "Eve Grinds Pigments for Artemisia Gentileschi," "Eve Condoles with the Rokeby Venus after the Suffragette Slashing," and "Eve and Psyche Arrive for a Shift at the Mirror Factory"

Indiana Review: "The Public Is Invited to See the Yew Trees in Full Fruit at This Time"

Juxtaprose: "To the man who tried to grab my face through the car's open window"

The Lindenwood Review: "Cary/Carrie"

Lines + Stars: "After the Exhibit"

The Louisville Review: "Nine Minutes in June"

Lunch Ticket: "Elementary"

Michigan Quarterly Review: "Reading Szymborska under a Harvest Moon"

The Massachusetts Review: "Eve Considers Cezanne's *The Basket of Apples*"

Nightjar: "April Ghazal"
Nimrod: "In Another Life, You Live"
On the Seawall: "Hip Check" and "Convent"
Pasque Petals: "*n* Miles from Wall Drug"
Pedestal: "Soon Enough"
Porter House Review: "Curation"
Radar Poetry: "In Shaker Heights They Culled the Elms"
Rogue Agent: "Hymn in My Sickness"
Scoundrel Time: "Election"
The Shallow Ends: "Midlife"
Shenandoah: "Do Not Fail to Yield" and "Questions about Bisexuals, #4"
The Shore: "Saint Agnes Meets a Hawk on the River's Edge"
sidereal: "Spectral Evidence"
Sixth Finch: "Skin"
Southeast Review: "My Son Asks if I Would Rather Live in a House Infested by Bees
    or a House Infested by Koalas"
Southern Indiana Review: "The Eider Keepers" and "On a school morning in
    mid-October"
Sugar House Review: "Somewhere a shark" and "In Your Copy of Akhmatova's
    Poems"
Tar River Poetry: "Playroom Canticle"
32 Poems: "Watertown"
Thrush: "No Names"
UCity Review: "Cigarettes after Sex"
The Worcester Review: "Rhododendrons"

"Spectral Evidence" appears in the anthology *The Ending Hasn't Happened Yet
    (Sable Books)*.

Some of the poems in this book also appear in the chapbooks *Dearling* (dancing girl
    press) and *Mirror Factory (Bone & Ink Press)*.

*

Reader, thank you for coming this far, and for staying just a moment longer, even
though mere language is inadequate to express my profound gratitude for the people
who have made these poems and this book possible:

Thank you to everyone at the University of Utah Press, especially Hannah New and Jessica Booth, for the care you've taken in shepherding this book into print.

Heartfelt thanks to Matthew Olzmann for spending time with this manuscript and for selecting it for the Agha Shahid Ali Prize—an absolute dream. Thank you for the further gift of your kind and perceptive words.

Thank you to Maggie Smith, Linda Gregerson, and Rachel McKibbens for encouragement when it was most needed.

For books and for refuge, I am grateful to libraries and independent bookstores, especially the Cuyahoga County Public Library, the Shaker Heights Public Library, the Montague Bookmill, Newtonville Books, the Watertown Public Library, and the Worcester Public Library. To the librarians at the WPL's Tatnuck Magnet branch: thank you for your dedication, enthusiasm, and forbearance with my unreasonably numerous holds.

Thank you to the poets of the Madwomen in the Attic and Fabrica Poetica for insight, compassion, and camaraderie. Thank you Emily Mohn-Slate and Julie Phillips Brown for your guidance, your poems, and the ways you welcome fellow poets.

In celebration and sorrow, I have been fortunate for the sustaining love and kindness of extraordinary friends. Thank you especially to Jenna Commito, Aaron Shapiro, Lindsey Gilbert, Katie DePasquale, Amy Stepsis, Elena Poillucci, Audrey Klein, Kate Dennis Nye, Thomas Dennis Nye, Heather Holcombe, Missy Hendrick, Joyce Fukami, Brian Woodrow, James Kocik, and Dean Lamsa.

Karen Van Cleve, for your blessing and for your magnanimous spirit, thank you.

For the sacrifices they made so that their children and grandchildren could thrive, I am indebted to my grandparents, sorely missed: Carol M. Batt, Ronald Batt, Jack Wilson, and Joyce Wilson.

For lifting me up countless times in myriad ways, thank you to my aunts, uncles, cousins, in-laws, and their families, including: Neil Batt, Jenny Michalski, Jack Batt, Penny Batt, Tom Batt, Galen Davis, Douglas Batt, Dominique Batt, Nancy Callas, Richard Callas, Heather Anderson, Nina Benegas, Nelda Hoxie, Liz Prager, and Sarah Prager.

I don't know if there's a collective noun for nieces, but I think it should be "gladness." Thank you Cora, Eleanor, Maren, Helen, Mollie, Bryn, and Lydia, my gladness of fierce and funny niecelets.

Ohio, the heart of it all: No matter the distance, I am so very grateful for the companionship of my siblings and their spouses. Thank you Claire Wilson, Julia & Jeremy Capetillo, and Tom & Jessica Wilson. To my parents, Raymond and Paula Wilson, whose voices were my first poems: I am humbled by your steadfast support. Thank you for your love, generosity, and patience.

Joy cometh in the morning, and Horatio, you are my morning star. It is the honor of my life to be your mother. Thank you for being your stellar self.

Benjamin, my love, my home and rest: for everything—but in this instance, for belief above all—thank you.